Transmutation

Poems by
Paula Camacho

BLUE LIGHT PRESS ✦ 1ST WORLD PUBLISHING

1ST WORLD
PUBLISHING

SAN FRANCISCO ✦ FAIRFIELD ✦ DELHI

Finalist, 2021 Blue Light Poetry Prize

Transmutation

Copyright ©2022, Paula Camacho

BLUE LIGHT PRESS
www.bluelightpress.com
bluelightpress@aol.com

1ST WORLD PUBLISHING
PO Box 2211
Fairfield, IA 52556
www.1stworldpublishing.com

BOOK & COVER DESIGN
Melanie Gendron
melaniegendron999@gmail.com

COVER AND INTERIOR ART
Melanie Gendron

AUTHOR PHOTO
Lorraine Conlin

FIRST EDITION

ISBN: 978-1-4218-3522-8

Praise for *Transmutation* by Paula Camacho

While the world outside knows "famine, pestilence,/ *wars and rumors of wars,*" Paula Camacho, with eloquent grace, invites us into her private sphere of transformation.

From inside her cottage, her garden, nature's bountiful beauty is a catalytic transformer – "birdsfoot violet, red trillium, pink bleeding heart" – so even if just for "a few tender moments," she knows tranquility, while "heaven and [she] connect."

She transforms in the grand peacefulness of a meditative state, where "mortality is an illusion," in "small wonders" of "simple moments," when her wakened eyes can find sunlight through shadows, and her "mind empties" with focused attention, as at a sparrow's "little leaps/ from shrub to magnolia tree." She even translates herself into a beach painting's "lone memory."

Love is one of her most important transformers, enabling her gliding across the pages of her life "as a brush/ flush with color." And then she dares directly gaze at dying, as a power saw removing a blistered cherry's branch "buzzes like the surgical tool/ used to remove [her] breast," and she achieves the ultimate transmutation, to "not fear/ the coming winter."

– Gayl Teller, Nassau County Poet Laureate 2009-11, Walt Whitman Birthplace 2016 Poet of the Year, Author of *Flashlight: New and Selected Poems* (WordTech/ Cherry Grove, 2019)

Paula Camacho's chapbook, *Transmutation* gives a fascinating glimpse of self-examination and insight through reflections and observations of nature. Her precise language paints vivid images bringing the reader into her observations and introspections portrayed in snapshots of flora, fauna, and landscape. Her words evoke an awareness from the reader felt by the perceptiveness of the writer. Read Paula Camacho's poems, feel the spirituality and experience *Transmutation* written on paper as well as your soul.

– Peter V. Dugan, Nassau County Poet Laureate 2017-19

Paula Camacho's poems present moments of quiet observation as the seasons change. Her lyrical descriptions of "begonias blooming around the house like a necklace" and " I see one lone magnolia blooming and rejoice" are original and emotional. Throughout her celebration of nature, she is acutely aware of the ending of things. This beautiful, sensitive collection was a pleasure to read.

– Evelyn Kandel, Nassau County Poet Laureate

The poems in Paula Camacho's book, *Transmutation*, invites the reader to share how the delicate balance of nature and the seasons of time interact and shape our everyday lives even to the moments of the extraordinary.

The opening poem, "Ideal Morning," shows, "It is on a wooden deck overlooking a broad blue lake where I stand with cup in hand, smile at the sun...leaves forming their robes of color in their summer wind...The poem ends with (her) realization, "The water waits for me to slip into cool arms and for a few tender moments heaven and I connect."

Every poem is a delight to your senses in its own unique way.

– Maria Manobianco – Art Teacher, Artist, Poet

Praise for *Transmutation* by Paula Camacho

While the world outside knows "famine, pestilence,/ *wars and rumors of wars,*" Paula Camacho, with eloquent grace, invites us into her private sphere of transformation.

From inside her cottage, her garden, nature's bountiful beauty is a catalytic transformer – "birdsfoot violet, red trillium, pink bleeding heart" – so even if just for "a few tender moments," she knows tranquility, while "heaven and [she] connect."

She transforms in the grand peacefulness of a meditative state, where "mortality is an illusion," in "small wonders" of "simple moments," when her wakened eyes can find sunlight through shadows, and her "mind empties" with focused attention, as at a sparrow's "little leaps/ from shrub to magnolia tree." She even translates herself into a beach painting's "lone memory."

Love is one of her most important transformers, enabling her gliding across the pages of her life "as a brush/ flush with color." And then she dares directly gaze at dying, as a power saw removing a blistered cherry's branch "buzzes like the surgical tool/ used to remove [her] breast," and she achieves the ultimate transmutation, to "not fear/ the coming winter."

– Gayl Teller, Nassau County Poet Laureate 2009-11, Walt Whitman Birthplace 2016 Poet of the Year, Author of *Flashlight: New and Selected Poems* (WordTech/ Cherry Grove, 2019)

Paula Camacho's chapbook, *Transmutation* gives a fascinating glimpse of self-examination and insight through reflections and observations of nature. Her precise language paints vivid images bringing the reader into her observations and introspections portrayed in snapshots of flora, fauna, and landscape. Her words evoke an awareness from the reader felt by the perceptiveness of the writer. Read Paula Camacho's poems, feel the spirituality and experience *Transmutation* written on paper as well as your soul.

– Peter V. Dugan, Nassau County Poet Laureate 2017-19

Paula Camacho's poems present moments of quiet observation as the seasons change. Her lyrical descriptions of "begonias blooming around the house like a necklace" and " I see one lone magnolia blooming and rejoice" are original and emotional. Throughout her celebration of nature, she is acutely aware of the ending of things. This beautiful, sensitive collection was a pleasure to read.

– Evelyn Kandel, Nassau County Poet Laureate

The poems in Paula Camacho's book, *Transmutation*, invites the reader to share how the delicate balance of nature and the seasons of time interact and shape our everyday lives even to the moments of the extraordinary.

The opening poem, "Ideal Morning," shows, "It is on a wooden deck overlooking a broad blue lake where I stand with cup in hand, smile at the sun…leaves forming their robes of color in their summer wind…The poem ends with (her) realization, "The water waits for me to slip into cool arms and for a few tender moments heaven and I connect."

Every poem is a delight to your senses in its own unique way.

– Maria Manobianco – Art Teacher, Artist, Poet

Acknowledgements

These poems first appeared in the same or similar form in the following publications:

"The Gift" in *Paumanok, Poems and Pictures of Long Island*
"Artemisia Caudata" in *Dream Long Island*

Contents

Ideal Morning

It is on a cabin's wooded deck
overlooking a broad blue lake
where I stand coffee cup in hand,
smile at the sun flickering through trees
the leaves fanning their velvet robes of color
in a summer wind.

The day ahead promising a walk
among the woodland wildflowers,
birdsfoot violet, red trillium, pink bleeding heart.
The water waiting for me to slip into its cool arms
and for a few tender moments
heaven and I connect.

The Gift

Scarlet cups of tulips
lifted high on spires
of green stems,
if I could paint beauty
like Monet
find the brilliant red
to capture
a delicate brief life,
leave impressions
on canvas
like water lilies
or crimson dotted red poppies
in a field of violet and green
where his wife Camille
and son Jean
still stand near,
if only the flux
and flow of words
stroked across
the page as easily
as a brush
flush with color,
what could I
leave of your essence
the love that fills me
the sweet smell
of red petals?

Transmutation

Sit in the softness of an evening sky
pretend mortality is an illusion.
Somewhere in the shadows under the oak,
around the lilac bushes, between the trunks of cheery trees
layers of life go on. The earth and the sun
and the rising moon eluding senses
caught in the footprint of stars. The day mellows
at their turn, slips so easily into night where
time does not separate spiritual from reality.
One day I will be gone from this beauty, perhaps
what remains will be seen by another
in the ochre of an evening sky.

Simple Moments

Sunlight strobes my eyes
as I drive through shadows of trees.

I am not looking for miracles
small wonders surround me –

the brown rabbit between my red petunias
the lavender lilacs scenting the air.

Poinsettias on my window
with lush greenery nine months past Christmas.

Last spring my magnolia tree suffers
fierce winds.
I watch her blossoms die.

Today, as fall approaches, I see
one lone magnolia blooming
and rejoice.

Sparrow

You return each day.
Your wings rippling over
a green shrub near the window.
My mind empties as I watch
your little leaps
from shrub to magnolia tree
to newly cut grass,
so carefree your motions
like ocean waves,
so comfortable your return each day.
I hear Mozart's Symphony
in your movements
and linger in my thoughts
about your finite being,
how your modest nature
can bring such peaceful moments.

Glorious Garden

I travel through
Pink Dogwood
Maidenhair Fern.

For days
I coil around
Goldenrod,
Joe-Pye Weed,
Edgeworthia
Winterberry Holly.

I have my choice –
Encore Azalea
Hydrangea.

Planting is
a mystical tour
of moistened earth.

Its damp aroma
an embrace
of inhaled pleasure.

Earth Day

Red breasted robin
I long to invite you to stay.

Like the dazzling blue jay
and blood red cardinal
you only visit
the ramparts of my house.

This year you cannot know
the magnolia blossoms are few.
Last year's winds took all
but the branches you rest on.

In the ever wave of life and death,
spring returns for the chosen few.

Outside there is famine, pestilence,
wars and rumors of wars.

For now we are safe
here in the sphere of my street.

Occupation

The scent of salt and sand
welcomes my morning.
My cottage doorframe
is an assemblage
of discarded creature homes –
Lion Paws Scallop,
ZigZag Scallop,
Rose Petal Tellin.
The more curvaceous ones,
Banded Tulip,
Wentletrap,
Lightning Whelk,
descend along wires like bells.
Village people call me
"the seashell lady"
but I do not sell them
by the seashore.
With basket in hand
my daily pursuit is
to hunt for empty shells
diligently searching
for my Angel Wings.

Artemisia Caudata

In the dunes at Wades Beach
Tall wormwood sway on sandy surfaces
Lime and chestnut feathery leaves join
In union together on tan beds
Tiny circular clusters like green grapes
Invite travelers to stop by
Their hubs deceptively hard
A gentle tug reveals an unyielding
Surrender to life hatched deep in the
Earth below as if clinging
Anchors its place in the universe
The soft black feather of a herring gull
Lays entwined in the plant
Casual remnant of a departed one

Lighthouse

– painting by Ryan Bowers

The sun drapes its evening light
on cottage and lighthouse
while brown slats of fence
hem in the sands below.
Pale blue lingers above
the amber wake of sky
creamed with clouds.

I feel myself walk into the scene
smell the salt of the sea
watch white foam sprawl across the shore.

The painting hangs on my wall
as a lone distant memory:
days at the beach
movement in the softness of a wavering earth,
lulled by a cool wind
into a meditation of beauty.

Summer Heat

I walk into humid air,
five seconds to collect the newspapers
that lay scattered over the driveway.

On return to the front door
I take a moment to admire
the pink begonia's bursting in full bloom
bordering the house like a necklace.

Trips to the ocean and beach
and beastly August heat will fade into cooler days.
Until then I will slide into the pool
watch the squirrels scurry to prepare for winter.

Cherry Tree

You are dying,
your bark blisters with age
like wrinkles on my hands.
Each year you hunch forward
closer to the earth.
Your leaves still green
tiny currant cherries
still produced
but today as if
too heavy to bear
a large branch
has fallen from you
prompting my husband
to buy a power saw.
It buzzes like the surgical tool
used to remove my breast.
I watch sweat pool
on his skin
see the long-branch
divided into cords.
It is the start of an end
we cannot avoid.

Wait

Trees are a crinoline of green.
Hyacinths huddle close to the fence.
Ivy climbs the cherry trees.
The oak stands alone
stretching its arms over all
like a mythical god.
Summer is
where a filigree of rain
refreshes in the hot sun.
I want to plead
for autumn to wait,
wait to change these lavish leaves
into their colorful charms.
Wait autumn!
Wait a little longer
before the applique
of winter snow.

Autumn Begins

At first the cold enters like an intruder
ready to rob long summer days.

It darkens the sky
turns leaves into old men
who scatter their drying flakes
over pale green grass.

It churns the oil burner
into phantom rumbles and thumps.

Soon the bushes are covered
with white fuzzy webs,
the yards turned into cemeteries
and clouds loom overhead like an omen.

Then the cold becomes a friend,
takes you in its arms
invites you to join in one season
dying into another with its brilliant
crimson and chestnut colors,
its orange pumpkin profusion,
its message that you need not fear
the coming winter.

Amaryllis in Winter

The plant sits in front of a window.
Its red petals stark against the snow sculptures
of bush and branch behind the glass.

A nymph full of unrequited love
asks the oracle of Delphi
how to capture the shepherd, Alteo's love.

She pierces her heart
with a golden arrow at Alteo's door
but when he opens it, a crimson flower is found.

Is it the storm that leads me to wonder about this bloom
or has this lone flower brought the snow to show
how affection still lives in the petals of a heart?

For the Anniversary of My Death

my dreams fade in the early morning light
where the wind whispers the blue song of memories

in the warmth of spring
In the lavender of the lilac

on dark and cloudy days
I will remember what has passed
and you will hear me in the soft strength of rain

About the Author

Paula Camacho is the President of the Nassau County Poet Laureate Society which selects and supports a Nassau County Poet Laureate every two years. She is a breast cancer survivor and participated in various poetry organizations over the years. She moderated the Farmingdale Poetry Group for 20 years. She taught a poetry class, *You Can Write Poetry*, in the Adult Education program at the Farmingdale High School. She served on the Nassau Council for the Arts for three years. Her poetry has won various awards, including the Alice Abel National Literary Contest and her haiku poems won first place for five consecutive years in the Performance Poets Association Haiku contests. Her published books include *Hidden Between Branches, Choice*, and *More Than Clouds*. She holds degrees in Nursing and Theology. Her email is PaulaCamF@aol.com

www.ingramcontent.com/pod-product-compliance
Lightning Source LLC
Chambersburg PA
CBHW021918040426
42447CB00007B/915